MYSTERIES
OF THE
CONSTELLATIONS

by Lela Nargi

CAPSTONE PRESS
a capstone imprint

Capstone Captivate is published by Capstone Press, an imprint of Capstone.
1710 Roe Crest Drive
North Mankato, Minnesota 56003
www.capstonepub.com

Library of Congress Cataloging-in-Publication Data is available on the Library of Congress website.
ISBN: 978-1-4966-8081-5 (library binding)
ISBN: 978-1-4966-8720-3 (paperback)
ISBN: 978-1-4966-8174-4 (eBook PDF)

Summary: What are constellations? Who named them? Where can they be found? Budding astronomers will learn all about constellations, including the history of studying the stars, how today's constellations were named, and how constellations help today's astronomers.

Image Credits
Alamy: Science History Images, 16; International Astronomical Union: M. Zamani, 22; iStockphoto: libre de droit, 21, TOLGA DOGAN, 11; Newscom: World History Archive, 12 (Inset); Science Source: Chris Butler, 25, David A. Hardy, 19, Jerry Lodriguss, 28, Larry Landolfi, 9 (Bottom), TIM BROWN, 17, Tim Vernon, 29; Shutterstock: Genevieve de Messieres, 27, Josep. Ng, 13, KoSSSmoSSS, 7, M Andy, 9 (Top), Martina Badini, 5, Masahiro Suzuki, 8, oxameel, 14, shooarts, 24, Taeya18, Cover, thipjang, 6; U.S. Navy: photo by Mass Communication Specialist Seaman Michele Fink, 10

Design Elements
Shutterstock: Anna Kutukova, Aygun Ali

Editorial Credits
Editor: Hank Musolf; Designer: Sara Radka; Media Researcher: Jo Miller; Production Specialist: Laura Manthe

All internet sites appearing in back matter were available and accurate when this book was sent to press.

TABLE OF CONTENTS

Words in **bold** are in the glossary.

CHAPTER 1

SHAPES ABOVE

The night is clear. You can see the stars. Some of the stars form patterns and shapes. The Big Dipper, the Little Dipper, and Orion are some of the most famous constellations.

Constellations help us make sense of the night sky. They can be used to guide people who are traveling. They let us keep track of time. But who discovered them? How do people use constellations to guess the future? How do astronomers use constellations? What mysteries of space can be solved by studying these star patterns?

Lascaux cave paintings

SEEING STAR PATTERNS

People have looked for patterns of stars in the sky for a long time. Different cultures throughout history found different shapes. A cave painting in France is 17,000 years old. It shows a rhinoceros constellation. A 6,000-year-old tomb in China held drawings of dragon and tiger constellations. The Mayans filled books with turtle, bat, and frog star shapes.

SAME STARS, DIFFERENT NAMES

Some cultures had different names for the same star groups. The Corona Borealis is also called the Northern Crown. Pawnee call it the Council of Chiefs. It contains the bright star Polaris. Pawnee call that the Star That Does Not Walk Around.

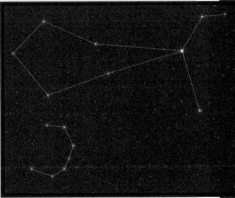

CHAPTER 2

WHAT'S IN A PICTURE?

Constellations are fun to spot in the sky. But they are also tools. Before calendars, people looked at stars to help them know when seasons would change. When Scorpio got two extra tail stars in spring, it was time to plant crops.

stars of Orion

Summer Triangle

The Summer Triangle meant it was time to harvest crops. Winter was near when Orion turned up. The stars helped farmers plan out their fields ahead of time. Some farmers still know these signs.

Orion

FINDING OUR WAY

Ship crews once used stars to find their way at sea. Sailors looked for the constellation named Cassiopeia. This helped them find the star Polaris. Polaris is between the Big Dipper and Cassiopeia. It is always in the north. That is why it is called the North Star. By finding it, sailors would know which direction they were going. Navies still teach sailors how to use **celestial** navigation.

A sextant uses the distance between its user and the stars to help sailors.

Birds use stars and the
moon for navigation.

CHAPTER 3

ANCIENT STARGAZING

Around 1200 BC, Babylonians and Sumerians mapped many constellations. They passed their knowledge to Romans and Greeks. A Greek scientist named Ptolemy wrote a book in AD 150. It named 48 constellations.

Twelve were **zodiac** constellations. Greeks and others thought the zodiac told the future. People today still read zodiac predictions. Your zodiac sign is based on the day you were born.

Ptolemy

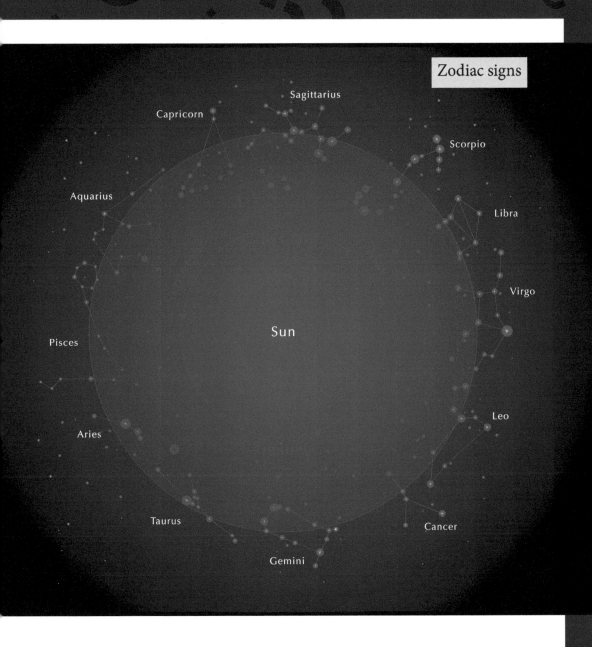

Sagittarius

Capricorn

Scorpio

Aquarius

Libra

Virgo

Pisces

Sun

Leo

Aries

Taurus

Cancer

Gemini

MYSTERY FACT

Telling the future from stars is called **astrology**.

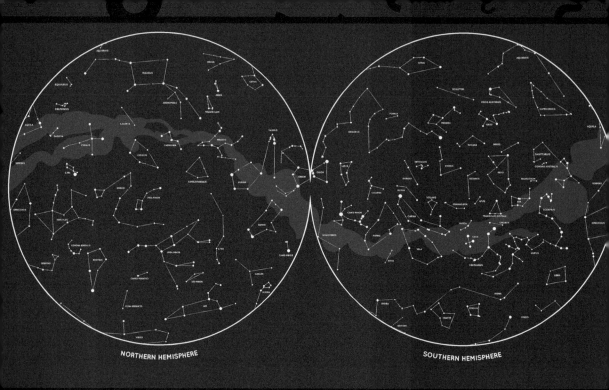

NORTHERN HEMISPHERE

SOUTHERN HEMISPHERE

MAPPING THE SOUTHERN SKY

Some early **astronomers** lived in the Northern **Hemisphere**. They could only see northern stars. They only mapped northern constellations. Northern people started to sail to the Southern Hemisphere in the 1550s. Aboriginal people already knew the stars there. Now Northern people got their first look.

CONSTELLATIONS

Some astronomers named constellations for kings. One English scientist named 13 constellations after toads, leeches, and slugs. None of these names stuck!

Discoveries are being made within the constellations today. Scientists discovered a black hole within Sagittarius. A **black hole** is a part of space with strong gravity that pulls in anything that comes close.

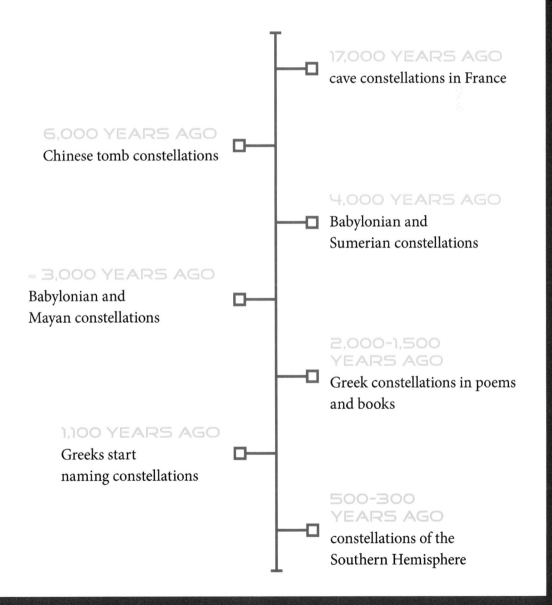

17,000 YEARS AGO
cave constellations in France

6,000 YEARS AGO
Chinese tomb constellations

4,000 YEARS AGO
Babylonian and
Sumerian constellations

≈ 3,000 YEARS AGO
Babylonian and
Mayan constellations

2,000–1,500
YEARS AGO
Greek constellations in poems
and books

1,100 YEARS AGO
Greeks start
naming constellations

500–300
YEARS AGO
constellations of the
Southern Hemisphere

CHAPTER 4

HOW CONSTELLATIONS "MOVE"

It looks like stars in constellations move. What we really see is Earth moving.

Our planet spins on its **axis.** One spin equals one day. Earth passes constellations as it spins. They seem to rise and set.

Our planet **orbits** the sun. One orbit equals one year. Different constellations come into view as we make this trip.

A **planisphere** is a wheel that helps locate constellations.

A celestial sphere is an imaginary sphere where constellations can be seen.

Some constellations are visible every night. Others only appear some nights. Scientists know which constellations will appear each night. They make maps of the sky that show which constellations you'll be able to see based on the time of year and your location.

CHAPTER 5

LOOKING DEEPER

The universe is expanding. Sky objects pull away from each other.

So stars do move, and constellations change shape. But we do not notice. The changes take hundreds of years.

Earth wobbles as it spins. This made seasons shift over time. We see the zodiac at different times now.

Let's go back 5,000 years. Spring came when the sun passed through Taurus. Now it comes when the sun passes through Pisces.

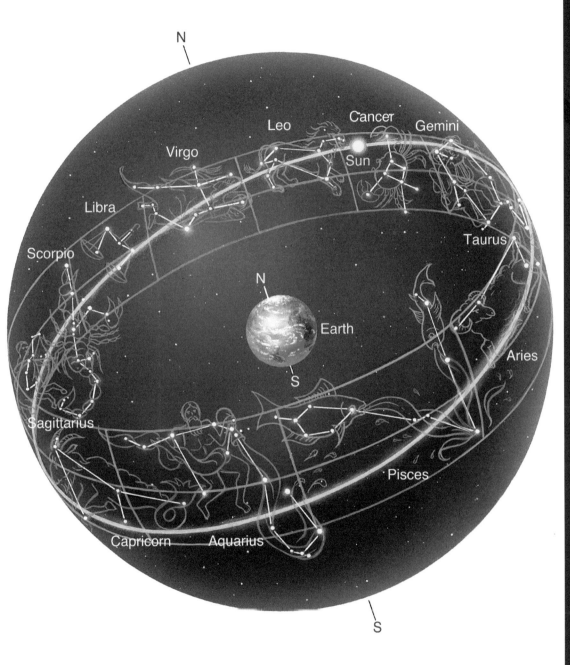

CONSTELLATION VS. ASTERISM

Some sky shapes are **asterisms**. Asterisms may have fewer stars than constellations. They have names. But astronomers do not officially recognize them.

An asterism may be part of a constellation. An example is the Big Dipper. It is part of the Great Bear constellation. The Northern Cross asterism is part of the Cygnus constellation.

Some asterisms span constellations. The Summer Triangle is made up of three stars. Deneb is in Cygnus. Vega is in Lyra. Altair is in Aquila.

MYSTERY FACT

Other names for the Big Dipper:

- The Plow, England
- The Saucepan, France
- An Emperor's Chariot, China

URSA MAJOR
THE GREAT BEAR

MUSCIDA

DUBHE

TALITHA

ALKAPHRAH

MEGREZ

ALCOR

MIZAR

ALIOTH

MERAK

PHAD

ALKAID

TANIA BOREALIS

TANIA AUSTRALIS

ALULA BOREALIS

ALULA AUSTRALIS

IT'S OFFICIAL

What makes a constellation official? The International Astronomical Union, or IAU, decides. The IAU is a group of astronomers. They name stars and explain the sky. They took 48 Northern Hemisphere constellations. They broke them into 50 constellations. They added 38 Southern Hemisphere constellations.

These are our 88 official constellations. We can see 60 in each hemisphere. We never see more than 24 at a time. The IAU calls every other star shape an asterism.

The members of the IAU vote to make decisions about constellations. .

CHAPTER 6

COUNTRIES IN THE SKY

As we have seen, IAU divided the sky into 88 pieces. They named each piece for its constellation.

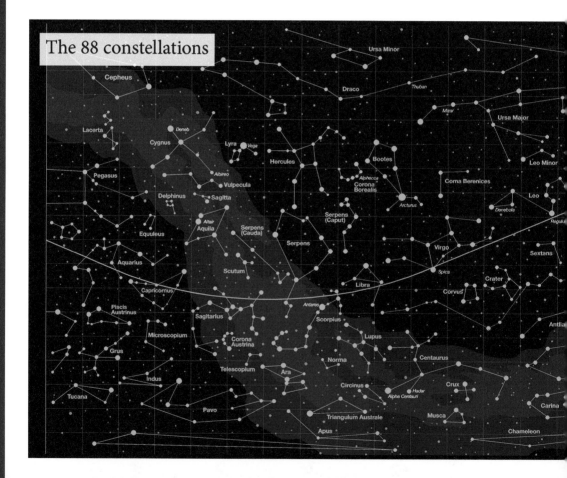

The 88 constellations

Imagine the 88 sky pieces are countries. Each country has borders. Inside its borders lies one constellation. The country is named after it. Orion, Leo, the Giraffe, and Draco are some constellation countries.

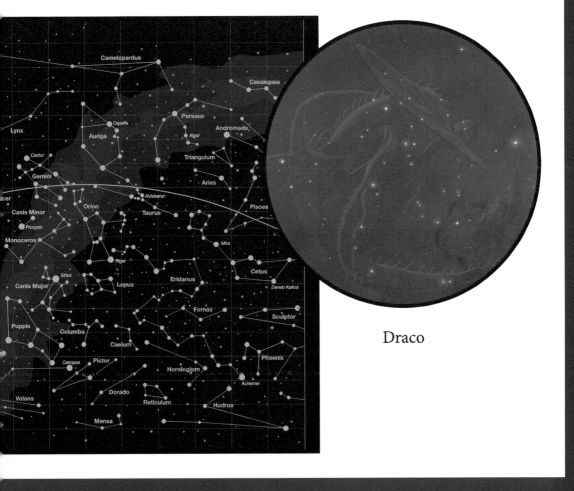

Draco

A JOB FOR CONSTELLATIONS

Constellations once had a job. People used them to navigate. Calendars and navigating tools took that over. We stopped using astrology as science. The IAU gave constellations a job again.

We first named stars we could see with our eyes. Then we invented telescopes. We could see even more stars. Now we find new stars all the time. We need an easy way to tell people where old and new stars are.

A star takes part of its name from its constellation. It takes part of its name from its brightness. Alpha is brightest. Omega is the least bright. The brightest star in Taurus is called Alpha Tauri.

MYSTERY FACT

Stars in a constellation are not the same distance from one another. Bright stars may be farther away than dim stars.

Taurus and the Pleiades
star cluster

CHAPTER 7

OLD IS NEW

Astronomers once used words from their own cultures to name constellations. **Archeoastronomers** study ancient sky cultures.

The IAU gives ancient names to some stars. Four stars now have Aboriginal names. And 86 stars now have Chinese, Hindu, Mayan, and Polynesian names. Astronomers continue to look for new discoveries wtihin constellations, like new black holes. They use advanced telescopes and other tools as they study the sky. What do you think they might find next?

Canis Major, the "Big Dog."

El Caracol Observatory helped the ancient Mayans study the stars to help with farming.

GLOSSARY

archeoastronomer (ar-KAY-oh-uh-strah-nuh-mur)—a scientist that studies the astronomical knowledge of ancient people

asterism (AS-tur-ism)—a small group of stars within a larger constellation

astrology (uh-STRAH-luh-jee)—the study of how the positions of the stars and planets affect people's lives

astronomer (uh-STRAH-nuh-muhr)—a scientist who studies stars, planets, and other objects in space

axis (AK-siss)—the pretend line that runs through the center of Earth; Earth spins around it

black hole (BLAK HOL)—invisible region of space with a strong gravitational field

celestial (suh-LESS-chuhl)—relating to the stars and the sky

hemisphere (HEM-uhss-fihr)—one half of the Earth; the equator divides the Earth into northern and southern hemispheres

orbit (OR-bit)—to travel around an object in space; an orbit is also the path an object follows while circling an object in space

planisphere (plah-NIH-spheer)—a sky map that lets you see what constellations are overhead at night

zodiac (ZOH-dee-ak)—the twelve constellations through which the sun, moons, and planets move each month

READ MORE

Oseid, Kelsey. *What We See in the Stars.* Berkeley, CA: Ten Speed Press, 2017.

Rey, H.A. *Find the Constellations.* Boston, MA: HMH Books for Young Readers, 2016.

Thacher, Meg. *Sky Gazing: A Guide to the Moon, Sun, Planets, Stars, Eclipses, and Constellations.* North Adams, MA: Storey Books, 2020.

INTERNET SITES

American Museum of Natural History: Ology Astronomy Page for Kids
https://www.amnh.org/explore/ology/astronomy/a-kid-s-guide-to-stargazing

Astronomy for Kids: The ABCs of Observing
http://www.astronomy.com/observing/astro-for-kids/2008/03/the-abcs-of-observing

NASA Science: Space Place
https://spaceplace.nasa.gov/

INDEX